WINDOW DECORATING

The Hunter Douglas Guide to

WINDOW DECORATING

The Complete Reference for Designing Beautiful Window Treatments

Text by Carol Sama Sheehan

Design by Paul Hardy

Principal photography by William Stites

Window treatments have evolved into an art form that superbly blends the practical with the aesthetically pleasing. On the cover, silky Silhouette window shadings are a subtle yet rich under-treatment for a luxurious drapery made from a Carole Fabrics selection; the same shadings at French doors preserve privacy and the stately decor of a traditional study, previous page. Opposite, Hunter Douglas vertical blinds offer a chic contemporary solution to light control. Following page, an elegant look is achieved by layering Austrian shades over Hunter Douglas pleated shades. Pages 8 and 9, Country Woods brings the classic qualities of wood slats to a modern bay window.

Published by American HomeStyle/The New York Times Company Women's Magazines, 110 Fifth Avenue, New York, New York 10011

Manufactured in the United States

ISBN 0-9636751-0-9

First Edition

FOREWORD

In recent years, no area of home design has undergone such dramatic change and diversification as the world of window fashions. Breakthroughs in technology and refinements in style have elevated the treatment of windows to an art, and Hunter Douglas has been the leader in the field.

The purpose of this book is twofold:

1) to introduce you to the multiple roles blinds and shades play in bringing privacy, security, energy efficiency, and beauty to windows in every room of a house, and,

2) to help you create, out of the myriad of choices available, the most stylish and practical window fashions for your own interiors.

As the Hunter Douglas Group looks forward to its 75th anniversary in 1994, we have much to celebrate. Hunter Douglas has developed from a small entrepreneurial company to the world's leading window fashions manufacturer. Our success is based largely on our reputation for style and innovation, in which we take great pride. Hunter Douglas is known for developing the first aluminum venetian blind in the 1940s. In the last decade, the company's growth has been phenomenal. During that time, we have brought a myriad of remarkable new products to consumers, most notably Duette honeycomb shades and Silhouette window shadings.

Today, Hunter Douglas Window Fashions is the premier producer of window coverings, offering under one banner an array of products ranging from honeycomb shades to pleated fabric shades, from horizontal blinds in aluminum and vinyl to fabric and wood blinds, from vertical blinds in fabric and aluminum to window shadings. To make the window an integral element of interior design, our line offers draperies, upholstery fabrics, bedspreads, pillows, table rounds, and decorative accessories that complement all Hunter Douglas window covering products, as well as hardware systems—in short, everything for the well-dressed window.

Some thanks are in order. Although our home base in North America is in Upper Saddle River, New Jersey, we presently employ some 8,000 people worldwide and operate more than 100 companies that market Hunter Douglas products in more than 80 countries. The ideas offered in this book represent the collective expertise and experience of all our employees. Special thanks go to Miriam Feinseth, our director of advertising and communications, for overseeing this project from conception to production. We would also like to thank the editors of *American HomeStyle*, a New York Times Company magazine, for their assistance in bringing our ideas to you in this beautiful and useful book.

Jerry Fuchs

JERRY FUCHS
PRESIDENT, HUNTER DOUGLAS

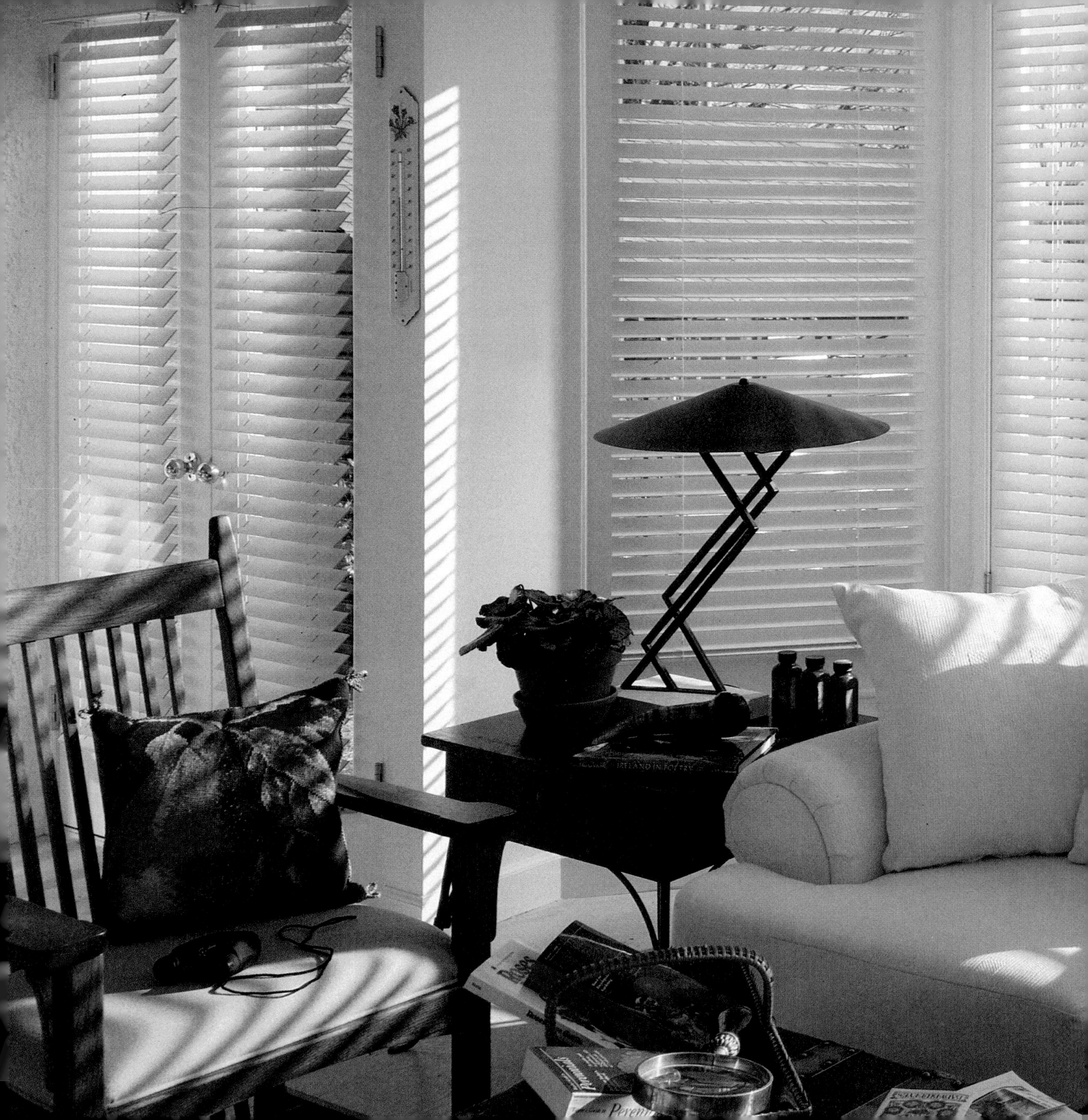
IRELAND IN POETRY
Roses

STYLE
AND DECORATION

Successful window treatments bring a combination of style and decoration to a room that is appropriate both for the visual setting and for the role of the room. While "style" usually refers to the overall look of a design scheme and "decoration" to its flourishes and details, these two elements are inseparable in the art of creating beautiful and enduring window fashions.

Window fashions have come a long way since animal skins and oilcloth were thrown across the tiny apertures that passed for windows in primitive dwellings. The word "window," from the Norse, literally means "eye of the house through which the wind enters." As early as the 17th century, glazed windows with small panes of glass began to grace homes in Europe and the New World, along with simple wood shutters and plain cloth curtains. Not until the advent of mass-produced glass in the 19th century, however, did windows become a universal luxury.

Since that time, all shapes, styles, and sizes of windows have emerged, and, along with them, an astounding variety of techniques and materials for enhancing windows. In recent years, the simultaneous rise of new technologies and the emergence of a cogent design philosophy for treating windows has made the art of window fashions just that—an art that can bring beauty and comfort to every room in your house.

Elaborate window decoration with ornate draperies, top treatments, and shades is a hallmark of Victorian design.

As with any domestic art, window fashions should serve both practical and aesthetic purposes.

The style in which you treat your windows will be determined in part by pragmatic considerations. The window type; the need to control light, heat, or cold entering from the outside; the desire for security, quiet, and comfort and privacy—all will affect the decisions you make about window treatments.

Important aesthetic factors will also influence the way you choose to dress your windows. The architectural style of the house often points the way to the most handsome and appropri-

ate window treatments. To be faithful to an old-fashioned Victorian house, for example, you might choose billowing curtains with swags, fringe, and lace panels. Or you might tone down the period display with a combination of wood blinds and loosely swagged top treatment. In a standard-issue city apartment, a luxurious balloon fabric shade over a translucent window shading system can establish a distinctive decor for the entire room. In a country home, wood shutters and ruffled valances might be most seemly for the heart of the home, the living room or keeping room.

The design of the room setting, including its furniture, must be carefully considered in planning new window treatments. With so many decorating choices today—from English country to Shaker, Arts and Crafts style to Bauhaus, postmodern to western—the world of window fashions has expanded to make it possible to coordinate any style you fancy.

In a sleek, contemporary room where light and space are the dominant elements, horizontal miniblinds hung floor to ceiling over the window area make a dramatic statement without being

Previous page, windows in the paneled library of a landmark house in Tuxedo Park, New York, are fitted with unobtrusive miniblinds from the Hunter Douglas Lightlines Designer Series that harmonize with the rich wood tones.

obtrusive. Palladian windows can be outfitted with cellular light-filtering shades customized to fit within each arch. For bay windows, another style that places a unique stamp on a room, vertical blinds are available that fit closely into the bend of the window and help you to make the most of the bay as well as project the right look. The process by which blinds and shades can be covered in any of a host of specialty fabrics makes myriad room schemes possible. And the tailored look of fabric-like shades complements virtually any home style or decor.

Sleek miniblinds, in a range of colors and finishes, are a popular choice in both traditional and modern settings. These perforated slats permit appreciation of the view even when shut.

The principal function of the room will also suggest the most logical solutions for its windows. Curtains, draperies, top treatments, and fabric shades add romance and intimacy in a bedroom. The home office, increasingly common, comes into its own as a comfortable sanctuary for work, with softer window treatments using fabric in subtle patterns and colors instead of the purely utilitarian and often sterile commercial office arrangements.

Given the sophistication and diversity of window fashions, you might think deciding how to treat your own windows will be difficult. The fact is, window fashions are responsive to the precise personal tastes in furnishings, fabrics, art, and collectibles that inform every room with style. There are "hard" window treatments, "soft" window treatments, and combinations of the two, offering beautiful solutions for windows of every kind.

Hard window treatments include shutters, shades, and blinds made of metal, vinyl, or wood. Hard treatments are often more utilitarian than soft ones, though they may also be decorative; they are appreciated for their simple, streamlined look and their capacity to control light.

Soft window treatments encompass draperies, curtains, soft shades, and top treatments and trimmings. (Although the terms "curtains" and "draperies" are sometimes used interchangeably, curtains are generally considered to be soft window coverings gathered onto a wood or metal rod, while draperies are pleated fabric coverings suspended by hooks from traverse rods or other carriers.) Soft treatments use fabric to enrich windows and rooms with color, pattern, and texture. Unlike hard treatments, they can carry out a room's decorative theme or pattern, add a generous note of opulence, and even stand on their own as major focal points of interior design.

Hard/soft window treatments combine elements of both types. Borrowing the best of both worlds often provides the ideal solution for window treatments. When the practical merits of blinds and shades are combined with the aesthetic benefits of fabrics, windows become much more than "the eye of the house through which the wind enters."

Formal treatments consisting of flowing draperies in rich textiles, large-scale swagged valances, and sheer curtains make these tall windows the focal point in an English-style drawing room.

A voluminous layered drapery treatment using luxurious fabrics and trimmings, left, is the kind of ball-gown dressing called for in a grand residence with wood-paneled walls and towering ceilings. The formally balanced swags and cascades are echoed by the sheer undertreatment. The fabric rosettes used in the top trimming and tie-backs are examples of the embellishment used with pleasing effect in Victorian and Empire window treatments. Above right, a single silk taffeta curtain, shirred on a rod with Roman shade undertreatment, provides dramatic window dressing for a highly stylized reading nook. A room filled with images of antiquity, below right, is graced by a drapery edged with Greek key trim and tied back for elegant effect. The Roman shade diffuses the light and also ensures privacy.

Roman shades with their simple, tailored look provide a sophisticated alternative to country curtains in a bungalow stripped down and furnished sparely yet with elegant touches. The subtle stripes at the windows in both the bedroom, right, and the dining room, left, introduce just the right amount of no-frills decoration for these interiors. Folds created when shades are raised soften the appearance of the plain window architecture. When lowered, the material flattens out to filter light and provide privacy.

In a dining room where American handiwork and craftsmanship impart a country theme, Country Woods with one-inch wood slats extend the warm, rustic look to a bank of windows. The blinds combine a pleasing visual effect with good sun protection.

Properly selected, window treatments contribute just the right combination of function and fashion to residential or commercial space. Vertical blinds, left, an architectural version of draperies that add height to a room, offer the ultimate in privacy and light control with vanes that traverse and rotate smoothly. When closed, the vanes overlap tightly to block out light. The fabric of flat Roman shades, right, which can be raised or lowered to take advantage of exterior light and views, filters incoming light to soften any interior. In this eclectically furnished living room, fabric for the shades was selected to coordinate with the existing decor.

Alternative treatments for the same window illustrate the wide range of practical and aesthetic features that can be incorporated into window fashions. Sheer curtains from Carole Fabrics combined with top-down crinkled cotton pleated shades, right, update windows in a traditionally styled room. Top row, left to right: The elegance of Silhouette window shadings softened with a swag in a Carole Fabrics cabbage rose print creates a decidedly romantic effect. Fabric vertical blinds combine the pleasing lines of draperies with almost total control of incoming light. Two-inch Country Woods with coordinating woven tapes provides a touch of relaxed formality with a Carole Fabrics curtain overtreatment. Bottom row, left to right: Pleated fabric shades paired with a shirred valance in the same watercolor pattern add drama to a spare country setting. Sleek miniblinds from the Lightlines Designer Series form a uniform backdrop for showing off eclectic furnishings. To cool down a hot Caribbean look, Duette Duolite combines two fabrics on one window for maximum privacy and light control—room-darkening Duette Eclipse in a rich purple on the bottom, translucent Duette Sheer Visuale on top.

Duette Elite honeycomb shades help to turn a bedroom into a romantic sanctuary, left, adding the warmth and texture of fabric to a window wall. When the shade is raised the fabric stacks compactly, leaving the window almost entirely in the clear. In a Southwestern boudoir characterized by strong architectural window elements, right, room–darkening Duette Eclipse keeps the desert sun at bay, at the same time adding its purity of line to the space.

In a converted barn with few sources of illumination, Duette Elite honeycomb shades permit filtered light to infuse the space with warmth. Matched with simple full-length curtains, they also provide an elegant backdrop to the rustic furnishings.

O pulent Austrian shades with their scalloped edges imbue a spacious country bathroom with Victorian romance, left and right. The fabric draws up into elegant folds, or ruches, across its entire width. Austrian shades can be made from a variety of fabrics, ranging from plain cotton ticking to delicate silks and sheers. In this room, a colorful chintz print was chosen as a tribute to the owner's passion for gardening and to coordinate with the blue-and-white theme of the pillows, porcelain, and floor.

In this contemporary house, the living room enjoys a southern exposure that is virtually a wall of glass. Pleated shades allow the view to be savored through a veil of gentle, light-filtering fabric. The top-down/bottom-up operation of the shade is a versatile feature. When raised from the bottom, the shade stacks compactly; when lowered from the top, it yields privacy. Its crisp pleating suits both modern and traditional interiors.

GARNISHING

White two-inch Country Woods achieves a sleek, contemporary look appropriate to a high-tech kitchen, left. Unobtrusive pull cords allow complete light control at each window. In a townhouse kitchen where neighbors are close by, above right, custom skylights flood the work area with plenty of light even when the wood blinds are closed for privacy. The stylish window surrounds were added to echo the dominant wood theme of the room and to make windows and skylights work together as an integral unit. Below right, a pair of windows in a tall kitchen gain visual emphasis with Roman shades in a strong vertical pattern and cheerful colors.

Tailored shades made of canvas from Carole Fabrics pull up from the bottom, rather than down as traditional shades do, to give this loft bedroom plenty of privacy without sacrificing natural light. The chrome bedstead and contemporary furniture invite an uncluttered window treatment style.

35

I n a grandly scaled bedroom, an expansive arched window is cut down to size by the addition of a swag. In combination with two-inch aluminum blinds by Hunter Douglas, this cleverly creates the impression of a pair of windows surmounted by a half-round left unadorned in order to serve as a constant source of natural light.

A converted barn's over-size, unusually tall windows called for the simple solution of Country Woods two-inch wood blinds. The color stain complements the old oak flooring while the horizonal slat pattern adds a linear dimension to a wall of whitewashed barn board.

WINDOWS BY
DESIGN

Just as a picture frame sets off a painting, a window enhances the view from within and without. The window's shape and style, and its purpose—to take advantage of great scenery, simply to admit light, to add architectural interest—help to determine the best treatment. The fine art of window decorating lies in serving good design where it is found, and in providing good design where it is lacking.

n the Middle Ages, the glazier's art produced windows of such beauty that when noble families moved from one castle to the next, they took their windows with them. Thanks to today's sophisticated window fashions, modern homeowners appreciate their windows almost as much, and with reason. Properly treated, window fashions play an important and sometimes dominant role in successful interior design, helping rooms to come alive with light, color, and character.

In designing new window treatments—light control and privacy being the primary concerns—it is helpful to evaluate each window to be treated in four ways: 1) as an individual unit, 2) in relation to other windows, 3) in relation to the style and design of the room itself, and 4) as seen from the outside looking in.

Taken individually, a window may first be identified by type; that alone often suggests the direction your window treatment should take. For example, French doors that swing open and patio doors that slide open require shades or blinds with different operating systems. Standard sash windows and picture windows lend themselves to

An arch window adds a note of charm and historic reference to a house's architecture.

a multitude of hard and soft solutions. The unique architectural details of arch and bay windows are greatly enhanced by the correct window treatment. Clerestory windows high on a cathedral ceiling or round porthole windows demand specialized yet effective treatments. There are equally effective custom solutions for skylights, conservatories, unusually shaped windows, and glass walls.

If the size or shape of an individual window is unsatisfactory, a fabric treatment can be devised to make it appear larger or smaller, taller or wider than it really is. In this way, the art of window fashions compensates for the deficiencies of style and function often found in older houses or those that have undergone awkward remodeling.

Just as a beautiful picture frame enhances a painting, window frames with distinctive structural features, such as pilasters, pediments, fanlights, or arches, add drama and distinction to the window. A window with a visually interesting surround would be treated differently—perhaps only with clean, unobtrusive blinds—than one with no distinctive architectural outline.

Evaluating the window's context yields other clues to the most appropriate way to treat it. In traditional houses, such as Cape Cods or Colonials, window placement is usually orderly and balanced, while in many new buildings, a random, even whimsical pattern is often the rule.

A window that stands by itself on a wall can be treated independently. Often, however, windows are hung in pairs or larger groupings, and a suitable treatment must encompass the set. If two windows different in height are paired on a wall, they can be trans-

Previous page, a casement window trimmed in a lively color is well served by Duette honeycomb shades that allow enjoyment of the view when raised. Left, a Duette Classic honeycomb shade lends itself to an elegant fan-like treatment for a half-round window.

formed into twins simply by mounting draperies and valances at a different height above each window frame, making the shorter window appear to be the same size as its taller neighbor. Similarly, adjacent windows can be made to appear as one by hanging draperies to conceal the wall space between them.

The most important step in designing window treatments is evaluating the window in relation to the style of the room setting. Formal rooms usually call for attention to detail at the window. Rich fabrics and elegant ornamentation help to bring such a room together in a harmonious decorative scheme. Informal rooms, however, may require simpler solutions. When furnishings are casual and unpretentious, unduly sumptuous windows run the risk of fussiness and overstatement.

Rooms with a period stamp generally benefit from window treatments that acknowledge the style. Ornate top treatments, such as pelmets or wood cornices with panels of rich brocade tied back with braid, would look out of place in a simple Colonial room but are authentic additions to one in an Elizabethan or Baroque style. When pelmets, cornices, or valances are used, an effective design for the top treatment may imitate one of the dominant shapes in the room, such as the outline of a fireplace mantel or sofa back. Similarly, fabric pat-

Duette honeycomb shades, here with Skyrise hardware, can be adapted to fit skylights and windows on angled walls.

terns used at the window can agreeably echo those found in a room's furnishings, promoting a cohesive design.

Historic accuracy is not always desirable in outfitting a room. In a true Victorian parlor, windows were covered with heavy draperies and large swags, but this decor produces a room most of us would find dark and depressing today. Today's Victorian-house dweller sensibly cuts back on period trappings, opting perhaps for lacy shades set into ornately carved surrounds.

Finally, it's always a good idea to visualize how treatments will appear from outside the house. Aesthetically, window fashions should go virtually unnoticed from the outside, yet contribute to the architectural character of the house. No single window should stand out, nor should drapery, blind, or shade colors clash with the building's facade. Windows adjacent to each other but treated in markedly different styles also distract from the house's appearance as a unified entity.

You needn't resort to an uninteresting uniformity in window treatments to achieve a design that's successful from inside and out. But the Mies van der Rohe dictum "Less is more" is worth heeding. Variations can be introduced from room to room and from floor to floor with considerable flair that accomplish your decorating goals without destroying the harmony of the exterior.

A custom-built house takes advantage of modern window design to exploit the natural light. Stylish window coverings have evolved to keep pace with these new specialty shapes.

A large fixed-glass window positioned to make the most of this beach house's ocean views is covered with Duette Sheer Visuale by Hunter Douglas, a knit fabric shade offering optimal transparency. The shade has been installed to permit raising from the bottom or lowering from the top. The same product, with its honeycomb construction, is versatile enough to cover specialty window shapes such as the room's porthole window as well.

Graceful arch windows, left, a focal point in almost any room, are often left uncovered if there is no need for privacy or light control. In this playroom, Duette Elite honeycomb shades meet practical needs without detracting from architectural beauty. The arch shades, which are movable for added light control, and the window shades are separate installations. Windows in a nursery, right, are covered with pleated shades in an appropriately whimsical pattern from the Hunter Douglas collection A Shade Younger. The addition of blackout backing on the shades makes the room sleepworthy at naptime. The circular window dressing is a stationary installation, while the conventional window shade can be raised or lowered.

The problem posed by the central tall glass doors in this formal entry hall was solved with the installation of Duette shades in a vertical orientation, known as Duette Vertiglide. When open, these shades compress to a mere six inches from a width of up to sixteen feet. The side windows are treated with the same product in a horizontal installation, to permit raising from the bottom or lowering from the top. The shirred-on-the-rod curtains in a floral from Carole Fabrics are accented with decorative tiebacks.

The unique curved-track Duette Smart Shade hardware system, which can be motorized, allows any curved window to be covered. A conservatory in a townhouse, left, relaxes in Victorian comfort under an arched greenhouse ceiling covered with Duette honeycomb shades on Smart Shade mountings. A simple remote control opens the room fully or partially to dramatic views of the sky. Right, the curved glass wall in a contemporary home spa is custom-fitted with Duette shades on the same mounting system.

Because of their slim profile and ease of operation, Lightlines Designer Series microblinds were chosen for light control in the glass–doored gallery of a newly built residence, in a color to complement the woodwork.

THE RIGHT
LIGHT

Natural light is the soul of a room, a tangible presence in house or workplace that allows occupants to experience the changing seasons and times of day. The amount of light appropriate or desirable varies from room to room. Window treatments help us to bask in the light, to artfully screen and filter it, and, when need be, to restrict it completely.

Wood blinds, as effective as metal or vinyl blinds in controlling light and privacy, also contribute the classic look of shutters.

Film directors and impressionist painters have at least one thing in common with successful window fashion designers—an understanding of light.

What moviegoer hasn't been affected by the dramatic lighting of a scene—afternoon sunlight streaming melodramatically through venetian blinds into the private eye's office, or a pair of lovers walking along a beach, romantically backlit by the setting sun? What museumgoer hasn't been transfixed before one of Monet's giant canvases, shimmering with enough light to nurture a thousand flower gardens?

The subtle yet powerful effect of light on human beings is just as noticeable in the private home . Windows and window fashions provide the means for us to use natural light in the most beneficial ways, enjoying it to the fullest, yet able to control it.

Make no mistake about it, light, especially natural light, makes us

Previous page, Hunter Douglas vertical blinds offer a practical yet handsome solution to minimizing the effects of strong sunlight on a family room's furnishings. The vanes traverse and rotate to keep the brightness in check, and stack compactly.

feel better, physically and emotionally. Usually without realizing it, we enjoy the changing conditions of light as each day and each season unfolds. For our sense of well-being and happiness, it is in our interest to bring as much natural light into our homes as possible. Window fashions help to light rooms in a way that is both practical and pleasing to the eye.

"Practical" cannot be overlooked, for a window full of light by day may resemble a black void by night, robbing the dwellers of privacy and making them uneasy. Blinds, shutters, shades, and layered fabric treatments restore a sense of security and intimacy without compromising the luxury of light by day.

The orientation of your windows, their size, shape, and placement, and the window treatments you select together determine how effectively natural light illuminates your interiors.

The direction your windows face—their exposure—is your first consideration. North-facing windows bring in the clearest, most even and consistent light, which is why this exposure is preferred for artists' studios. This light has a cool, bluish cast. In northern climates, builders limit the number of windows on the north side because it is the coldest exposure. For energy conservation, those windows are often treated with insulated fabric shades, shutters, lined draperies, and cornices.

East-facing windows admit warmer, brighter light, especially in the morning. For this reason, these windows are often treated with materials that diffuse the light, such as pleated shades, sheers, woven blinds, and shutters.

Windows that face west are exposed to the hottest light—and also the haziest, due to the fact that by day's end, there are so many more impurities in the atmosphere. Because prolonged exposure to this strong light can be damaging to wood furniture and colored fabrics, especially in summer, west windows are generally covered with any one or a combination of light-diffusing treatments, including vertical or horizontal blinds, pleated shades, shutters, and sheers.

South-facing windows, the most important natural-light source in any building because they receive sunlight year-round, cast a warm, golden glow on interiors. Again, some combination of light-diffusing window treatments helps protect fabric and furniture in rooms on that side of the house.

The manner in which natural light comes into a room is also affected by window location. Windows high on an exterior wall admit light deep into the room, while low or wide windows bring in the light in shallow swaths. In small rooms, the presence of several windows will offer a more even distribution of natural light; so will groupings of windows in a large space.

Light also falls into a room in colors and patterns that are affected by the exterior atmosphere and landscape and by window treatments themselves. Shimmering puddles of summer light, filtered through a tree's foliage onto a floor, add a romantic dimen-

The opaque Duette Eclipse shade, here in a bottom-stacking configuration, provides light-filtering shade by day, right, and blackout-dense privacy by night, left.

sion to a living room. The same effect is felt when light pours through lace curtains, shutter louvers, or the slats of blinds.

Materials selected for window treatments can harness natural light to pleasing effect. When sunlight streams through diaphanous fabrics or translucent pleated shades of white, rose, or yellow, the room is cast in similar hues. For a window with an unsightly view, a pleated shade combining translucent and opaque fabrics draws in light by day and protects privacy at night. In bathrooms, opaque coverings such as wood blinds, miniblinds, shades with privacy backings, or window shadings all provide elegant solutions. In an east-facing bedroom, room-darkening shades, accompanied by pretty curtains or draperies, block out dawn's early light but permit warm afternoon light to flood the room.

A new generation of skylights and greenhouse windows offers dramatic ways to incorporate natural light into home design. Master bedroom spas, sun porches, atria, and conservatories all have gained charm and livability from the advanced technologies in treatments for such windows. Miniblinds, louvered shutters, and fabric shades with built-in insulation provide stylish systems for controlling light, ventilation, and exposure to cold air in winter climates, or for basking in full sun in the interior space.

A Silhouette window shading imparts the warmth of gently diffused light to a formal room setting, with an asymmetrical drapery to add a dramatic touch.

As the dramatic focal point in a formal setting, a towering wall of glass brings architectural interest and abundant natural light into a room. Elegantly simple sheer fabric Silhouette window shadings, installed on the glass doors, uniquely combine the functions of shade and blind. They permit an unobstructed view when open, yet safeguard privacy when closed.

Light is controlled at a tall window in a modern room setting, left, with sleek horizontal aluminum miniblinds from the Lightlines Designer Series that seamlessly integrate a curved headrail and valance with the spring-tempered slats. Right, two banks of café shutters were installed in an imposing oversize window, creating a checkerboard of light and dark when opened at random. Lace draperies of uncommon beauty transform the window seat into a regal setting.

Pleated shades from Hunter Douglas ensure privacy for a bedroom, left, without depriving the occupant of light streaming through the leaded glass panes. A Carole Fabrics chintz overtreatment adds a welcome splash of color. In an old-fashioned kitchen where sunlight is important and the view is not, right, vertical blinds act as a privacy screen without intruding on the charm of the room.

A semitransparent honeycomb shade with the crisp look and feel of linen is well suited to a stylish interior with oversize windows. When extended, the two-inch pleat of Duette Majestic lies flat on the side facing the window and maintains crisp pleats on the room side. When raised, the entire shade stacks up out of sight so that the view is not obstructed.

An assortment of small, fixed-glass windows in a corner apartment in a high-rise, left, required a uniform and understated treatment. Two-inch Country Woods with a sandblasted finish blends with the walls when closed, takes advantage of sunny days when opened. Above right, aluminum horizontal miniblinds by Hunter Douglas are an eminently practical yet handsome solution for French doors in a master bedroom. The arched windows above the doors are covered with a shirred curtain fabric to let in light and coordinate with the pretty patterns about the room. For a remodeled Victorian attic space with a fabulous city view, below right, a minimal window treatment was most appropriate. Country Woods with two-inch wood slats and a sandblasted finish allows occupants to make the entire wall a window on their world, or to seal the room in comfort and privacy.

COLOR
PATTERN AND TEXTURE

The height of window decoration occurs when the richness of fabric and other materials is introduced. Not all windows call for opulent treatment, but when it is appropriate, the window can become a compelling statement. The orchestration of color, pattern, and texture, echoing the room decor and tempered by natural light, brings the window to its fullest realization as an expression of design.

The amount of decoration appropriate to a window depends on the role it serves in the room setting. That may be a subordinate, supporting, or starring role.

The window plays a subordinate role in the overall decor, for example, when the view it affords is so desirable—a cityscape by night, a beautiful garden or a patch of countryside—that to treat the window elaborately would distract from the vista. Such a window should be dressed so simply, with neutral lines and color the same as the wall, that the entire treatment recedes into the background. In a subordinate role, the window says, in effect, "Look through me."

In a supporting role, by contrast, it says, "Look at the room." When the window plays this role, it receives a higher degree of decoration in order to link it visually to the architectural style or interior design. More fabric is incorporated to coordinate with the fabrics and furnishings in the room.

Pleated shades in a range of hues and metallized fabrics offer many options for colorful, coordinated looks.

In a starring role, as a major focus within the room, the window declares, "Look at me!" Generally, windows are called upon to serve as focal points in rooms otherwise devoid of a visual center of attention. A room with a handsome fireplace or wonderful works of art probably doesn't need to have its windows singled out for lavish treatment. But a room lacking distinctiveness can be transformed by using dramatic or beautiful window fashions.

No matter what role a window is given, the judicious use of color, pattern, and texture is crucial to the success of its treatment. These are the three building blocks of window style.

Treating a window, in this sense, is not unlike coordinating a wardrobe. It involves the same concern for comfort, good taste, and fashion that dressing suitably for a particular occasion demands. Just as a person dresses in different ways for different occasions, windows call for a variety of styles. Some windows are meant to remain discreetly in the background and are dressed accordingly in a minimal or neutral style, comparable to conservative business attire. Others are the visual centerpiece of the room and deserve the same attention as the wardrobe mistress gives to her diva on opening night.

A more formal house and lifestyle will entail window fashions of greater sophistication and complexity than an informal abode. In choosing fabrics, formality is evoked with shimmering silks and taffetas, informality with soft cottons and polished chintzes. Sensitive choices produce sensible solutions.

Wood shutters add character and coziness to a room enjoyed as a library or family room. These may be stained, or painted to coordinate with any wall color in the rainbow.

Horizontal and vertical blinds are available in a wide spectrum

---

Previous page, the use of Hunter Douglas pleated shades in a rich tone, from the Kashmir collection, updates a chic 1920s European color palette. Right, the impact of color on a room is most dramatic when it is boldly stated. Duette Elite in a deep hue envelops a study in jewel tones.

of colors and textures. Miniblinds in metallic finishes are right at home in any sleek, high-tech interior. Wood blinds come in a range of natural finishes and fashion colors and combine effectively with curtains, draperies, and top treatments. Vertical blinds impose a handsome, drapery-like pattern on a window and, with fabric vanes, become draperies themselves, coordinating with other fabric patterns in the room.

Pleated shades, a relative newcomer in window fashions, are among the most versatile coverings available. They come in hundreds of colors and fabrics, allowing you to bring the look of lace, linen, silk, or even satin to your windows. Cellular shades provide a seamless honeycomb texture with marble, granite, and many other faux finishes. Another innovation, window shadings, combines the softness of a fabric shade with the function of blinds in a range of light-filtering colors.

Soft window fashions offer the most opportunity for asserting personal style. Unlike hard treatments, which are limited to the dimensions of the window frame, soft treatments, especially curtains and draperies, can be used to surround the window and create a dramatic focus.

Fabric shades bring the visual and tactile properties of textiles to windows and can be used in a multitude of settings. With their voluminous pleats and poufs, Austrian and balloon shades have a sumptuous, billowy style all their own, bringing opera-house elegance to a living room or bedroom. Roman shades have a crisp, tailored profile and can be as decorative as the pattern of the fabric they are made from. Most important, they are a means of introducing bold or subtle touches of color, texture, and pattern.

A large-scale floral combined with a stripe and a subdued damask, all from Carole Fabrics, produces a feminine look.

Top treatments and trimmings are decorator touches that customize and add interest to window fashions. Valances and cornices incorporate many different materials—wood, ironwork, fabric—and can be trimmed with such textural flourishes as welting, piping, gimp, braid, and fringe. Fabric valances can be shirred and shaped, pleated and tabbed. Wood cornices can be upholstered, painted, or antiqued.

Monochromatic color schemes using neutral colors are the safest and simplest to devise. A creamy white pleated shade with a lacy texture might be paired with beige curtains in a room with beige walls. In a more formal setting, a monochromatic scheme might be employed to visually outline a window with curtains, passementerie, and fringe, with matching undershade.

A coordinated color scheme might link a window treatment with an interesting upholstery fabric. A paisley padded valance could complement the paisley on a sofa, for instance, set off by wood blinds in the same background color found in the print. In a contrasting color scheme, English country chintz bedroom curtains and a sheer balloon shade might be paired with a slipper chair upholstered in stripes. Or, in a richly paneled room, a window might be hung in deep-toned draperies and crowned with an asymmetrical swag and jabot in a complementary color.

One of the most enduring fabric top treatments for windows has been the swag and jabot, a means of imparting style in varying degrees of formality. In this library where fine surfaces predominate, the silky fabric ties in with the texture as well as the color scheme. Country Woods blinds were selected in a stain to complement the woodwork. The one-inch slats provide a sleeker and more elegant look than wider slats.

In a bedroom with neutral-patterned walls and upholstery, left, the eye gravitates to the windows where 1940s-inspired print fabric combines with colorful Country Woods blinds to set the retro tone. Yellow tape on the wood slat blinds adds an unexpected spark to the mix. Right, various textures add interest to the soft palette in a living room with sponge-painted walls and translucent Fabrette fabric blinds. The addition of an Empire-style swag top treatment with irregular cascades and side panels provides a luxurious frame.

Bold blue miniblinds by Hunter Douglas, above, match the color scheme in this cheerful child's room. An ingenious installation of Hunter Douglas vertical blinds, right, turns one room into two. When closed, the blinds effectively close off the "bedroom" from the child's play area. On the windows, pleated shades in the same playful Dinosaurs pattern can be adjusted for privacy.

Today's color palette in aluminum blinds allows fully coordinated room decorating schemes. Bright gold miniblinds with one-inch slats from the Lightlines Designer Series, left, serve as an unobtrusive background in a room designed for restful contemplation. Right, pale pink microblinds from the same series, with half-inch slats, blend pleasingly with the wall color.

An elaborate fabric valance complete with swags, jabots, and flowing draperies, combined with a veil-like Silhouette shading undertreatment, transforms a wide dining room window into a feast for the eyes.

THE GUIDE

Window fashions and treatments are decorating tools for solving the problems and making the most of the opportunities that exist at every window. Everything you need to know in order to choose appropriate and attractive coverings for your own windows is summed up in this section. The Guide answers your questions, identifies your practical needs, and shows how to bring comfort, style, and personality to windows of every shape, size, and location in your house.

In an 1881 Victorian interior designed by Louis Comfort Tiffany, the layered look of the day was achieved with elegance through exotic print draperies, sheer curtains, a privacy shade, and a colored glass transom.

CLASSIC WINDOW TREATMENT STYLES

Spanish Colonial (1492–1850) freestanding shutters with handwrought screens combined the practical need to control light and heat with the beauty of Moorish design.

The **Renaissance** (ca. 1400–1600) saw a resurgence in the use of classical Greek and Roman forms at the window, notably in columns, pilasters, and cornices enhanced by rich fabrics in vivid colors. During the **French Renaissance** (1589–1643), windows were highlighted by heavy velvet or brocade draperies trimmed lavishly in gold braid. England's **Late Medieval Renaissance** (1558–1649) featured Gothic windows with heavily leaded glass in diamond patterns. Curtains were strung by means of attached metal rings on metal or wood rods close to the glass, with solid wood shutters to help keep out wintry air.

The reign of the "Sun King," France's Louis XIV, during the **Baroque** period (1643–1730) was marked by much ornamentation and elaborate furnishings. Vivid hues, opulent fabrics, and rich textures characterized treatments for windows. Draperies were tied back low and given heavy fringe and elaborate top treatments. In the **English Baroque** or **Early Georgian** (1660–1714) period, heavy cornices at the ceiling and the puddling of draperies on the floor denoted wealth and extravagance.

American Early Georgian (1700–1750), a scaled-down version of English Baroque, saw windows covered with raised panel shutters, both for privacy and insulation, as well as minimal swag-and-jabot-type overtreatments.

In the **Late Georgian** period (1751–1790), the rich reds, golds, and blues of the Chinese Chippendale style, in both imported and domestic fabrics, became the vogue. Draperies were fringed and tied back with tassels, and wood-slat venetian blinds began to gain in popularity.

The **Federal** period (1790–1820) introduced silk brocade, taffeta, satin, and voile to home interiors, hung asymmetrically and topped with swags. Upholstered, straight, narrow cornices and double-tieback treatments were commonplace.

The **Victorian Age** (1837–1901), along with the Industrial Revolution, produced a new class of nouveau riche, globe-trotting Americans, who brought back architectural ornaments and antiquities from their travels abroad to the Orient, Egypt, and Europe. These multiple influences were expressed in a cluttered, eclectic style reflected in ostentatious window fashions. Interiors were darkened by an abundance of generous swags, layers of lace, and voluptuous overdraperies.

Sumptuous fabrics embellished with decorative passementerie and rope–like metal tieback holders denote the luxurious style of French Empire window fashions.

Post-Victorian window treatments in the early decades of the century embraced the leaner "form follows function" ideology of the German Bauhaus and International movements. Curtaining and shading were downplayed as light itself became the primary element in defining window areas.

In the 1930s, **Art Deco** marked a return to glamour and elegance in the home. Full, tailored overdraperies had high tiebacks and sleek decorative rods and other hardware that reflected the interests of the times, such as Egyptian motifs.

In the **postwar era**, the color spectrum of window fashions evolved from drab to dusty to brilliant. Scandinavian design inspired the use of printed fabrics in long and short draperies. The plate-glass window was introduced as a popular form, and the first spring-tempered aluminum blind came on the market, as did vertical blinds.

Following the psychedelic excesses of **the 1960s**, a revival of traditional colors and styles was observed as authentic early American window treatments were devised for newly restored homes. At the same time, a contemporary, clean look became popular as sleek miniblinds moved from the workplace to the home. A few years later, an opulent English country chintz was one of the most popular window fashion statements of **the 1980s.**

A Hollywood bedroom of the early 1940s shows the sleek, sophisticated, elongated lines ushered in by the Art Deco and Bauhaus movements. Boldly striped draperies at the window and door reiterate the horizontal lines of the era's newly popular venetian blinds.

The antithesis of Victorian ornamentation, above, is found in the streamlined vertical blind window treatment of a contemporary interior, below.

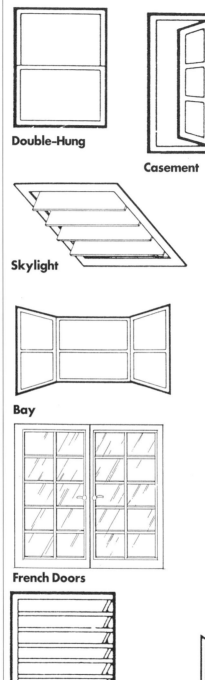

Double-Hung

Casement

Skylight

Palladian/Arch

Bay

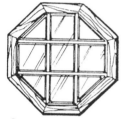

Octagon

French Doors

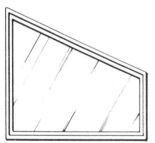

A-Frame

Jalousie

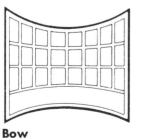

Bow

WINDOW STYLES

A glossary of common and specialty window styles.

A-Frame — a large window with an angled top that follows the line of a slanted roof or ceiling.

Bay — three or more windows set at angles to each other within a recessed area.

Bow — a curved window that forms an arc extending outward from the wall.

Casement — a crank-operated window that opens either inward or outward.

Clerestory — a shallow window set near the ceiling.

Corner — two windows that meet in a corner.

Dormer — a small window projecting from the house in an alcove-like extension.

Double — two windows set side by side, usually double-hung.

Double-Hung — a two-sash window in which one or both sashes slide up and down.

Eyebrow — a half oval or ellipse, often installed as a dormer.

French/Atrium Doors — a pair of doors with glass panes; with French doors, both sides open; only one door opens with atrium style.

Gothic Arch — an arch formed by a concave and a convex curve meeting in a point at the top.

For hard-to-reach rectangular windows, such as this pair of skylights, the Duette shade with Simplicity hardware is the answer to controlling light from above. The shade opens and closes with the aid of a handle and skylight wand.

Greenhouse — curved vertical windows that form both the walls and the ceiling of a sunroom.

Jalousie — narrow, horizontal slats of glass maneuvered by a crank.

Octagon — a modified circle formed of eight sides of equal length; a hexagon has six sides.

Palladian/Arch — a classical window form distinguished by its graceful arch.

Picture — a wide window designed to frame a view; usually a fixed center glass pane with side windows that open.

Ranch — a wide, high-off-the-floor window with sliding sashes.

Skylight — a window inserted into the roof or ceiling.

Sliding Glass Door — a modern version of the French door with two or three large panes, at least one of which slides to open.

ENERGY EFFICIENCY AND ROOM COMFORT

Many window styles call for energy conservation measures to reduce heating and air-conditioning costs and to assure that a room is as comfortable as possible for its occupants. Blinds and shades, on their own or in combination with curtains and draperies, can be selected for their special ability to insulate from the effects of heat and cold. Reflective metallized finishes such as Thermostop, available on several colors of Hunter Douglas aluminum blinds, and blackout linings

A custom dormer window playfully echoes the architecture of the house while helping to illuminate a dark alcove.

Tall casement windows frame a spectacular view in a pleasingly simple grid.

A round window with a ship's wheel pattern adds interest to a peaked roof facade and light to an attic.

on shades are two of many options that help to reduce energy loss. Another option, the honeycomb shade, has a cellular construction that traps air and acts as an insulator. Double and triple honeycomb styles create additional air pockets for even greater efficiency. The Phenomena 3 triple-cell shade from Hunter Douglas, with its resistance-to-heat-loss rating (R-value) of 4.8, is regarded as the most energy-efficient shade available.

In a room where Palladian windows are the focal point but the view is not, Duette honeycomb shades with a Duolite hardware system screen the view and make the best of the light. Two different shades—one sheer, the other blackout—operate from the same moving center rail with individual controls to allow flexible adjustment for privacy and light.

CREATING WINDOW FASHIONS WITH BLINDS AND SHADES

The classic looks and down-to-earth practicality of blinds and shades make them ideal choices for bringing a sense of style to both modern and traditional interiors. In design language, a blind is a tailored window covering consisting of horizontal slats or vertical vanes, which can be opened and closed, made from sturdy materials such as aluminum, vinyl, or wood. A shade is a window covering made from soft fabric or fabric-like material, thus lending itself to a broad range of decorative styles. It most commonly rolls or folds up from bottom to top.

Both the streamlined design of blinds and the visual softness of shades offer beauty and function in a neat package; each is capable of standing on its own or combining with lavish layers of draperies and top treatments for a highly personalized window statement.

Horizontal blinds are the contemporary version of the venetian blinds that date back to the 17th century. The blind consists of slats that can be stacked up by means of a pull cord. Another control allows tilting the slats for as much light control and privacy as desired.

Versatile horizontal blinds can be used alone, with top treatments, or as undertreatments in combination with draperies, and can be manufactured to fit almost any size and shape of window. They are available in aluminum, wood, vinyl, or fabric slats.

Aluminum blinds come with slats ranging from micro (1/2") to mini (1") to broader (2") widths. Their clean-lined design makes them suitable in almost any room decor. They are particularly compatible with modern architecture. Miniblinds can be cut to fit around air conditioners and window cranks, and custom-fitted to

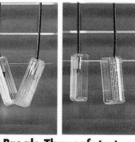

The Break–Thru safety tassel snaps together neatly, left, but opens under pressure, right, in case children get entangled in the cord.

unusual window shapes. Stacking space for aluminum blinds is minimal; a 6' blind stacks to less than 6" fully raised. Dozens of enamel finishes offer colors that coordinate with fabric styles, faux finishes, wood tones, or metallics. Duotone blinds combine a decorator color on one side of the slats with a neutral color on the other so that the closed blinds present a uniform exterior appearance. A special safety feature of aluminum blinds is the Break-Thru tassel available in the

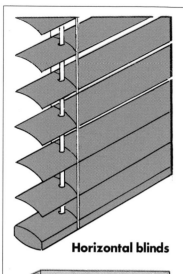

Horizontal blinds

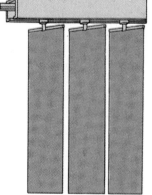

Vertical blinds

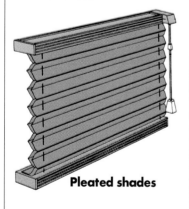

Pleated shades

Pleated fabric shades from the Hunter Douglas A Shade Younger collection bring crisp definition and a sense of humor to the windows of a playroom.

Vertical blinds from Hunter Douglas add height to a room visually, as well as providing excellent light control with vanes that traverse to open and rotate to overlap tightly.

Lightlines Designer Series, which snaps open under pressure to help prevent injury if a child or pet is accidentally caught in the blind cord.

Wood blinds, valued for their handsome, natural look, durability, and insulating properties, come in 1" and 2" slat widths. More expensive than aluminum blinds, the best wood blinds are made of basswood and are kiln-dried to prevent warping, splitting, or twisting. Finishes include traditional wood stains as well as washed and painted looks. Their woven cloth tapes come in coordinating or contrasting colors.

Vinyl blinds are a cost-effective alternative to aluminum and are made in a 1" slat width. High-gloss and pearlized finishes are among the most popular looks.

Translucent fabric blinds are a unique alternative to standard blinds. The fabric slats, which are available in the 1" size, filter the light in a room. Room-darkening fabric slats are an optional feature.

Vertical blinds, first introduced in 1948, are now available in a full range of finishes and textures, from moderately priced vinyl and aluminum to top-of-the-line fabrics. With vanes that traverse and rotate smoothly, they offer the ultimate in privacy and light control. Among Hunter Douglas products, aluminum verticals may be cross-matched with aluminum horizontals, and fabric verticals with pleated shades, for a coordinated look.

The vertical line of these blinds complements most window shapes and adds height to a room. Used alone, with valances or fabric top treatments, or as drapery undertreatments, they suit most decorating styles beautifully. Special track systems even permit verticals in bow, bay, and angled window installations.

Verticals "stack," or compress, tightly when opened, taking up much less space than draperies. When closed, the vanes overlap closely, keeping out heat in summer and cold in winter. The vertical position of the vanes prevents dust from collecting—gravity does the job of dusting for you.

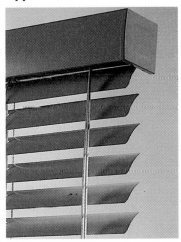

Fabric verticals come in a broad range of colors and textures.

The sleek profile of Lightlines Designer Series spring-tempered aluminum blinds is achieved by a curved headrail. It functions as a built-in valance to conceal brackets and to project an all-in-one appearance at the window.

Vinyl verticals are made from sturdy PVC that will not twist or bow with age. Vinyls come in both neutral and vivid colors and a variety of textures and finishes. There are even sculptured vinyl louvers that create distinctive shapes and patterns, ideal for contemporary interiors.

clear grooved edges. Inserts also allow you to display a neutral color scheme on the outward side seen through the window and a different decorator color on the room side.

Pleated fabric shades first came to this country from the Netherlands in the 1970s and are now one of the most popular window fashions, lending their crisp, stylish look to any window as a solitary treatment or in combination with draperies. A 6' fabric shade stacks to under 3", making this an ideal undertreatment for draperies that virtually disappears when raised. The permanent pleats come in 1" and 1 5/8" widths. The shade's separate backing layer offers

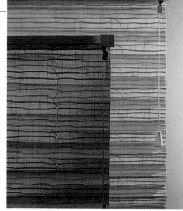

The crinkled cotton of sophisticated, contemporary pleated shades softly diffuses light and adds textural interest at the window.

high energy efficiency, complete control of light and privacy, and a uniform exterior appearance with a choice of room-side colors.

Metallized pleated shades are available in transparent, sheer fabrics that

allow light in or semiprivate fabrics that softly diffuse light by day and add privacy by night. They are very energy-efficient, reducing heat loss in winter by as much as 50 percent and heat gain in summer as much as 80 percent. Also, bonded aluminum backing on metallized pleated shades filters the sun's rays and helps prevent fading of carpets and furniture.

Nonmetallized pleated shades come in a choice of interesting fabrics including lace and eyelet, and in textures that evoke silk, linen, and even satin. Many are available with matching cut yardage fabric to create coordinated accessories.

The versatile pleated fabric shade is equally at home on standard, irregular, and special-shape windows, and in various unique applications. Two fabrics can be combined in one shade, one installed above and the other below a traveling center rail, allowing you to choose a sheer for day or an opaque fabric at night with the pull of a cord. Multiple shades may be hung from one headrail, an ideal solution for sliding glass doors and extra-wide windows; each shade can then be raised or lowered independently.

Fabric or wallpaper strips inserted into clear-edged groovers combine fashion and practical benefits in vertical blinds.

Aluminum vanes have baked enamel finishes for long-lasting brightness, plus the added benefits of easy maintenance and moderate prices.

Fabric verticals add a touch of warmth and softness to the window treatment. Free-hanging fabric vanes are weighted to maintain straightness. Fabric insert verticals use strips of the fabric of your choice inserted into solid vinyl backings with

The wide 2" pleats of this Duette honeycomb shade, which filters light through color, are aptly scaled to a large window. When the shade is lowered, the back flattens out against the glass, while the room–side pleats remain crisply in place.

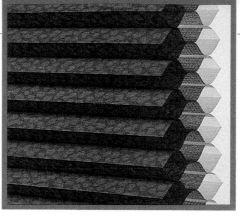

Duette Phenomena 3 honeycomb shades, shown here in a print that creates a dappled light pattern, are highly energy-efficient.

Cellular shades,

introduced in 1985, are made in a unique pleated construction resembling the honeycomb of a beehive, an important energy-saving feature. The fabric can be used either horizontally in widths of 3/8", 3/4", or 2", or vertically in the 3/4" or 2" widths.

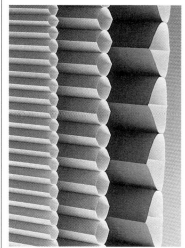

Three pleat sizes—3/8", 3/4", and 2"—make Duette honeycomb shades suitable for nearly any window style.

The tailored look of this window covering complements most window styles, from simple casements to challenging bows, arches, and angled tops. It can be used alone, with a simple top treatment, or under full draperies.

Flexible tracking systems enable these shades to fit the tight radius of bay or greenhouse window curves, as well as skylights. Raising or lowering large shades is simplified by a clutch-and-pulley headrail system, operated manually or motorized. To mount cellular shades vertically, an adaptable hardware system such as Duette Vertiglide is ideal for sliding glass or French doors.

Fabrics come in a wide spectrum of colors, including prints with marble, granite, or other faux finishes. The softness of the fabric combined with crisp pleating yields a look equally at home in traditional or modern interiors. Cellular shades are often used as a contemporary alternative to sheers. They offer as much or as little privacy as desired, with styles that are transparent, semitransparent, translucent, or completely room-darkening.

Window shadings, the newest fashion on the block (they were introduced in 1991), and one of the most intriguing, combine the softness and delicate light-filtering translu-

An alternative to draperies, Duette honeycomb shades combine the softness of fabric with the crisp look of pleats, above. Another choice, Silhouette window shadings, below, offers light-filtering qualities plus the functionality of blinds.

In a Shaker-inspired interior, Duette honeycomb shades with their unobtrusive design are a simple yet effective window treatment. The translucent fabric is sheer enough to permit light through without sacrificing privacy.

Colorful
tone-on-tone
stripes such as
these from Carole
Fabrics, above, are
versatile decorating choices. Below, Silhouette window shadings provide the luminous undertreatment for a large window adorned with valance, draperies, and shade in a striped fabric.

Balloon shades, above, combine the privacy of blinds when lowered with the beauty and fullness of draperies when raised.

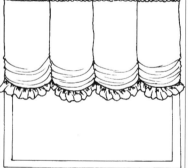

Balloon shade

cence of fabric with the functional abilities of a blind.

The shading consists of softly colored vanes of woven fabric suspended between two sheer knit facings. The entire system can be raised or lowered with control hardware concealed within the aluminum headrail, which can be mounted either inside or outside the window frame. The fabric slats, which tilt to permit an unobstructed view or close for privacy, are completely concealed when raised.

Because window shadings function like blinds, filter light like shades, but allow for as much privacy or view as desired, they have a broad range of applications. They work especially well on windows where the beauty of the light-filtering fabric can be appreciated. Window shadings can be used alone, with simple top treatments, or with draperies.

Fabric shades, offering the elegance and romance of custom soft shades, originated in Europe, with some of today's most popular styles dating back to the 1800s. The three most versatile fabric shades are balloon, Roman, and Austrian.

Balloon shades, combining the privacy of blinds with the beauty and fullness of draperies, are cherished for the distinctive billows that form as the shade is raised. The box-pleated balloon shade has a more tailored appearance, while the softer shirred shade is more feminine.

Balloon shades can be made of soft, drapable fabrics as well as crisp, lightweight ones. They can be used on their own as operating shades, in lieu of sheers with tied-back draperies for a rich, layered look, or as stationary valances.

A fully decorated girl's bedroom window combines an Austrian shade, shirred-on-the-rod curtains, coordinating tiebacks, and a matching ruffled valance.

Roman shades are simple, flat fabric shades that draw up in neat, even folds rather than in poufs, giving them a tailored look suitable in all decors—traditional, contemporary, transitional, or country. A softer version has horizontal folds across the full width of the shade to create texture and dimension even when the shade is fully lowered. Both styles can be fabricated as operating shades or as stationary valances. They look best in crisp, medium-weight fabrics.

Austrian shades are found in formal, elegant settings because of their rich appearance. This style of soft shade is generally made with 2-to-1 fullness

A delicate Austrian shade adds a romantic dimension to a bathroom overlooking a secluded garden, above, offering some privacy without obscuring the window's pleasing architectural lines.

across the width and 3-to-1 fullness in length. The extra volume creates a scalloped bottom and elegant ruching across the face of the shade. Sheer fabrics are the most popular choice for Austrian shades, but they can also be striking in cotton prints and other medium-weight fabrics, especially when used as valances.

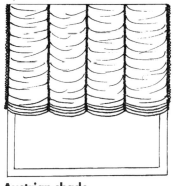

Austrian shade

The Coordinates Etcetera collection makes it possible to create a completely integrated look of made-to-measure top treatments for Hunter Douglas shades and blinds, as well as matching table skirts, pillows, slipcovers, bed covers, and more.

THE COORDINATED LOOK

A room comes together stylistically when all the aesthetic components are successfully blended. The palette of colors in the room is enriched and reinforced when textures and patterns in complementary hues are added through coordinating fabrics. In designing window treatments, as well as in choosing upholstery, slipcovers, pillowcases, and bed coverings, the key to successful mixing and matching is balance and understatement. Follow these guidelines:

● Choose a major print compatible with room elements (a curved pattern to echo curved furniture shapes, say).

● Let the dominant print be your road map for the room design, defining the color scheme and coordinates.

● Use no more than four patterns.

● Choose a secondary pattern smaller in scale than the dominant print; any additional pattern should be even less emphatic and of similar design.

● Good coordinates for large patterns are stripes, plaids, tone-on-tone designs, and textured effects.

● Simple paisleys mix well with geometrics such as stripes and checks, if they share common colors.

● Two prints work together when there is some relationship in pattern, theme, or especially color.

DRAPERY ABCs

The terms "draperies" and "curtains" are often used interchangeably, but each has different characteristics. "Drapery" describes a pleated fabric usually meant to be drawn open or closed by means of a pull cord, while "curtains" refers to fabric that is shirred or gathered onto a rod. Both draperies and curtains require a range of hardware, encompassing everything from rods to decorative tiebacks, holdbacks, and swagholders, for hanging and creating a customized appearance.

Traverse rod — the conventional hardware along which draperies move with the pull of a cord. When draperies are closed, rod is hidden; when opened, rod is visible unless concealed by top treatment. Drapes can either draw one way or split-draw from the center.

Decorative traverse rod — an inexpensive alternative to top treatments; rod, rings, brackets, and end finials are mounted to be visible above the drapery heading.

A French tassel combined with a holdback.

Hand traverse rod — available in a variety of styles and sizes, including wood poles and metal café rods. Drapery hangs below rod from rings and is opened by hand.

Shirred drapery rod — an acrylic or metal rod or wood pole that is threaded through a "casing" or "rod pocket" in the drapery heading to create a gathered or shirred look.

Tieback — a piece of fabric cut in any of several styles (straight, contoured, braided, gathered, etc.) that is used to hold a drapery panel back; draperies look best when tied back about a third of the distance from the top or the bottom of the treatment.

Holdback — a piece of decorative hardware that performs the same function as a tieback.

Swagholder — special hardware that allows fabric to be swagged in innumerable ways by pulling it through an open loop.

CUSTOMIZED TOPPERS

The area above the window treatment can be the room's crowning glory, depending on how you top it.

Heading — the top portion of a window treatment; various looks can be achieved by tabbing, pleating, or shirring.

Top treatment — any of a wide range of fabric treatments, primarily decorative, that literally crown a window arrangement. It can be used alone, over a blind or shade, or as the finishing touch to custom draperies.

Passementerie like this colorful cording and the trimmings at right, from Carole Fabrics, add a decorator flourish to fabric treatments.

Valance — a top treatment constructed from fabric; it may be flat, pleated, or gathered, and may hang from a board or a rod.

Cornice — a top treatment constructed on a wood frame, padded and covered with fabric.

Lambrequin — a padded, fabric-covered top treatment constructed on a wood frame, similar to a cornice, but with legs that extend to the floor.

Swag — a top treatment with fabric that falls gracefully from the top of a board or a pole, looping downward and then back to the top; several swags can be overlapped on wide windows and combined with cascades or jabots for decorative effect.

Trimming — any of a broad range of rich embellishments for top treatments, known as passementerie. These include fringe, tassels, braid, cording, and gimp.

Scalloped-bottom valance

Passementerie   **Shaped ruffled valance**

Shirred-on-the-rod valance

Decorative traverse rod

Conventional traverse rod

Standard decorative holdback

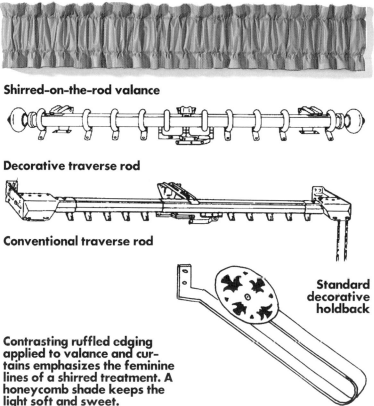

Contrasting ruffled edging applied to valance and curtains emphasizes the feminine lines of a shirred treatment. A honeycomb shade keeps the light soft and sweet.

In a monochromatic color scheme, texture provides a subtle point of interest at the window, where light is softly filtered through the fabric slats of Fabrette blinds.

PLANNING WINDOW TREATMENTS

ELEMENTS OF DESIGN

Space defines the boundaries and sets the limits on the area to be decorated. The space most directly affecting window treatments is the area immediately surrounding the window, including the wall and the window itself.

Key Questions

• Is there enough wall space to extend the treatment comfortably beyond the window?

• Is there so much space above the window that your treatment should encompass that space?

• Is the space so limiting that the treatment must be installed on or very close to the frame?

Space-Altering Solutions:

• A room that appears small looks best with a simple window treatment that blends with the walls and creates the perception of greater space.

• In an oversize space, a multilayered treatment helps give the impression of a cozier, warmer room.

Line, straight or curved, is the beginning point of all design. Straight lines include horizontals, diagonals, and verticals. The mood of a room can be altered by observing some guidelines:

• Horizontal lines create a sense of breadth, width, and size.

• Vertical lines add height, dignity, and formality.

• Diagonal lines attract attention and lead the eye, but they need to be sup-

ported by verticals or opposing diagonals so as not to be disturbing.

• Curved lines are romantic and feminine. They are used to soften or relieve straight lines in a room.

Window-Altering Solutions:

• Full side-panel draperies combined with a beyond-the-frame cornice can make a narrow window seem wider.

• A short window can be made to appear taller with the addition of an above-the-frame valance in combination with floor-length sheers and tied-back side panels.

Form is the result of lines joining to produce an overall shape. You can alter or emphasize the shape of a window by the treatment you select.

Windows come in all shapes and sizes, but most finished window treatments are rectangles. The straight lines of a rectangle can be softened with a gathered heading or the gentle folds of a swag and jabots. Conversely, the rectangular form can be emphasized with vertical banding or stationary side panels of fabric.

Texture refers to the surface quality, whether rough or smooth. Smooth, shiny surfaces are more formal; rough, coarse surfaces more casual. The use of a combination of textures in a room adds variety, but one should dominate. A room decorated primarily in slick,

shiny textures needs rougher textures for contrast and variation.

Choosing Textured Fabrics :

• Texture alters the color of fabric. A nubby fabric has shadows, which makes the fabric look darker. Shiny fabrics reflect light and appear lighter to the eye.

• Shiny fabrics, because they are reflective, also recede; coarse fabrics absorb light and appear to take up additional space in the room.

• While a combination of textures adds interest to window treatments, sharp contrast in texture should be used only for dramatic effect.

• Window treatments of nubby, coarse fabrics look best at 2-to-1 full-

---

One effective use of color at the window features Country Woods chosen in a finish to contrast with the background color of the wall and with tapes that coordinate with the upholstery.

ness. The reduced fullness accommodates the bulk of the fabric and minimizes the visual weight of the finished treatment.

PROPORTION AND SCALE

A window treatment pleasing to the eye obeys classic principles of proportion and scale:

● The placement of tiebacks affects the visual weight of a window. The correct placement is a third of the distance from either top or bottom.

● Use top treatments that are approximately one-fifth of the total treatment length.

● If cascades are not floor-length, they should fall even with another design feature such as a windowsill, chair rail, or muntin.

● Avoid hanging draperies with no visual reference point. Whenever possible, line up their hems with a windowsill, apron, or floor.

● In determining the scale of window treatments, their actual size as well as their visual weight should be compatible with other furnishings in the room

COLOR

The most important single element in decorating a room, including its windows, is the effective use of color. When selecting colors for window fashions, keep in mind:

● The unchangeable elements in the room, as dictated by budget, aesthetics and structural limitations.

● The size of the room.

● The location/exposure of the room.

● The amount of natural light.

● The room's function.

● Who will use the room.

● The decorating style desired.

The visual effects of color used in a window treatment will vary according to many factors:

● A brightly colored window treatment against a light background advances and fills the space. The same treatment against a dark background will not look as large or bright.

● A brightly colored treatment against walls of a lighter value of the same color will appear to blend in with the walls.

● To draw attention to a window treatment, use a bright color against a lighter value of its complement. To minimize the treatment, surround it with colors of the same value.

● Medium-value prints against a white background are easy to see at a distance; in neutrals, the same pattern is less eye-catching.

● The surface of a fabric affects its color intensity. A slick, shiny fabric such as satin or chintz will look more intensely red than the identical red on homespun linen.

● Subtle color contrasts make a room feel formal, calm, feminine. Bold color contrasts make a room feel informal, cozy, masculine.

● Color affects the appearance of lines. Horizontal lines in any color widen a window treatment; vertical colored lines against a contrasting ground add height.

● Warm colors visually advance, cool colors recede.

● Balance colors throughout the room. One hue should cover as much as two-thirds of an area, with a second color covering nearly a third.

A prominent window is integrated into the color scheme of a family room with Duette honeycomb shades.

Other colors act as accents. Repeating colors around a room or using a progression of values of one color—light green for walls, darker greens for draperies, furniture, and carpet—creates visual rhythm.

RESOURCES

A directory of Hunter Douglas window fashions products. For more information about these products, call 1-800-937-7895.

Horizontal Blinds

Lightlines Designer Series™
Flexalum® Decor®
Sunflex®
Celebrity®
Thermostop®
Country Woods™
Fabrette™

Vertical Blinds

Pleated Shades

Cellular Shades

Duette® honeycomb shades
Duette Chinoise™ (3/8" pleat)
Duette Classic™ (3/8" pleat)
Duette Eclipse™ (blackout shade, 3/4" pleat)
Duette Eclipse II™ (blackout shade, 3/8" pleat)
Duette Elite™ (3/4" pleat)
Duette Expressions™ (3/4" pleat)
Duette Imprints™ (2" pleat)
Duette Majestic™ (2" pleat)
Duette Phenomena 3™ (triple honeycomb)
Duette Phenomena 3 Celestial® (triple honeycomb)
Duette Phenomena 3 Constellation® (triple honeycomb)
Duette Sheer Visuale™ (3/4" pleat)
Duette Splendor™ (2" pleat)
Applause™ honeycomb shades

Window Shadings

Silhouette® window shadings

® A registered trademark of Hunter Douglas

™ A trademark of Hunter Douglas

Fabrics

Coordinates Etcetera™
Carole Fabrics

Hardware Systems

Duette Duolite™
Duette EasyRise™
Duette Simplicity®
Duette Skyrise®
Duette Smart Shade®
Duette Vertiglide®
Easy Glide™
Permaclear™
Permalign™

Safety Products

Break-Thru™ miniblind safety tassel

CREDITS

Special Consultants

Martin Lipsitt
Elizabeth Jane Pavelle

Copy Editor

Joal K. Hetherington

Contributing Photographers

Jean Mitchel Allsopp
pages 20-21

Laurie Black
pages 28-29

Karen Bussolini
pages 30-31

Jerry Cailor
pages 41 bottom, 55 top, 94 top

Culver Pictures
pages 82-83 bottom, 83 top

Gary Denys
pages 40, 68

David Glomb
page 38

Steve Gross/Sue Daley
page 59

John Hall
pages 14-15, 86-87 bottom

Brian Haviland
page 24

Jenifer Jordan
pages 90 top left, 91 bottom center, 93 bottom

Oleg March
pages 34-35

Keith Scott Morton
page 33 bottom

Bill Rothschild
page 90 bottom

Iggi Ruggieri
page 92 top

Michael Shopenn
page 33 top

Walter Smalling, Jr.
page 89 bottom

William Stites
cover and pages 2, 4, 7, 10, 22-23, 30-31, 46-47, 50-51, 52, 56-57, 60-61, 66, 69, 72, 76-77, 78-79, 80

UPPA Limited, London
page 48

Visual Concepts, High Point, NC
pages 8-9, 18-19, 25, 26-27, 32, 36-37, 41 top, 42-43, 45, 49, 62-63, 64-65, 70-71, 73, 74, 75, 84 bottom, 85 bottom, 87 top left, 88 bottom, 94-95 bottom

Dale Wing
pages 16-17

Bruce Wolf
pages 44, 58, 68-69 bottom, 86 top, 95 right

Architects

Austin Patterson Associates
page 59

Abraham Rothenberg
pages 30-31

Interior Designers

Perry Bentley
pages 20, 21

Sig Bergamin
page 15

Jeffrey Bilhuber
pages 34-35

Geoffrey Bradfield of Jay Spectre, Inc.
page 90 bottom

Arnold Copper
page 14

Mariette Himes Gomez
pages 30-31

Christine Maly Designs
pages 10, 46-47

Pamela Pearce
page 33 top

Ron Rezek
page 38

Jody Rose
pages 28-29

Susan Thorn
pages 2, 7, 50-51, 52, 56-57, 78-79

Nancy Wing
pages 16-17

Stylists

D. J. Carey
pages 22-23

Color Consultant for Hunter Douglas

Barbara Schirmeister

Project Assistant

Gina Harrell

Illustrations

Victoria and Albert Museum
pages 12 left, 82 top

We would like to thank the following companies:

DIA showroom, High Point, NC
page 4

Lillian August Collection, Westport, CT
pages 22-23

New Glass
pages 76, 77

Pella
pages 22, 40, 85 top left to right

Palazzetti
pages 76, 77